IT'S TIME TO EAT SEAFOOD SALAD

It's Time to Eat SEAFOOD SALAD

Walter the Educator

Silent King Books
A WhichHead Entertainment Imprint

Copyright © 2024 by Walter the Educator

All rights reserved. No part of this book may be reproduced in any manner whatsoever without written per- mission except in the case of brief quotations embodied in critical articles and reviews.

First Printing, 2024

Disclaimer

This book is a literary work; the story is not about specific persons, locations, situations, and/or circumstances unless mentioned in a historical context. Any resemblance to real persons, locations, situations, and/or circumstances is coincidental. This book is for entertainment and informational purposes only. The author and publisher offer this information without warranties expressed or implied. No matter the grounds, neither the author nor the publisher will be accountable for any losses, injuries, or other damages caused by the reader's use of this book. The use of this book acknowledges an understanding and acceptance of this disclaimer.

It's Time to Eat SEAFOOD SALAD is a collectible early learning book by Walter the Educator suitable for all ages belonging to Walter the Educator's Time to Eat Book Series. Collect more books at WaltertheEducator.com

USE THE EXTRA SPACE TO TAKE NOTES AND DOCUMENT YOUR MEMORIES

SEAFOOD SALAD

It's time to eat, let's all sit down,

It's Time to Eat
Seafood Salad

Seafood salad's the talk of the town!

Fresh from the ocean, tasty and light,

A meal that's healthy and just right!

Shrimp so pink with a little curl,

They make your taste buds dance and twirl.

Crab so sweet in every bite,

Seafood salad is pure delight!

Flaky fish, both soft and mild,

A flavor treat that makes you smile.

Octopus slices, tender and neat,

A special surprise in every seat!

Add some lettuce, crisp and green,

With cucumbers fresh and shiny sheen.

Tomatoes juicy, so red and round,

A mix of flavors that will astound!

It's Time to Eat
Seafood Salad

Drizzle some lemon, sour and bright,

A zesty twist that feels just right.

A sprinkle of herbs, a pinch of spice,

Seafood salad is oh so nice!

Fork in hand, take a bite,

Feel the ocean, pure delight.

Each little taste is fresh and new,

Seafood salad is good for you!

Share it with friends, pass the dish,

A meal like this is everyone's wish.

Eating together brings such joy,

For every girl and every boy!

Morning, noon, or evening meal,

Seafood salad has great appeal.

It's nature's gift, from sea to plate,

It's Time to Eat
Seafood Salad

A dish to love, it's truly great!

One last bite, then we'll say,

"Thank you, sea, for a lovely day!"

Fresh and yummy, tried and true,

Seafood salad's the best for you!

So let's all cheer and shout hooray,

Seafood salad brightens the day.

Healthy, tasty, and oh so grand,

It's Time to Eat
Seafood Salad

A feast of the sea, right in your hand!

ABOUT THE CREATOR

Walter the Educator is one of the pseudonyms for Walter Anderson. Formally educated in Chemistry, Business, and Education, he is an educator, an author, a diverse entrepreneur, and he is the son of a disabled war veteran. "Walter the Educator" shares his time between educating and creating. He holds interests and owns several creative projects that entertain, enlighten, enhance, and educate, hoping to inspire and motivate you. Follow, find new works, and stay up to date with Walter the Educator™ at WaltertheEducator.com

www.ingramcontent.com/pod-product-compliance
Lightning Source LLC
LaVergne TN
LVHW052014060526
838201LV00059B/4037